My Buddy K
LETTERS!

Volume 1

My Buddy Knows Series

A
B
C

Keith Wheeler

My Buddy Knows Letters

By Keith Wheeler

From the My Buddy Knows Series, Volume 1

This book is dedicated to my loving family.
You inspire me to be a better writer and a better person, each and every day!

This is my buddy, Josh! Josh knows a lot about...

LETTERS!

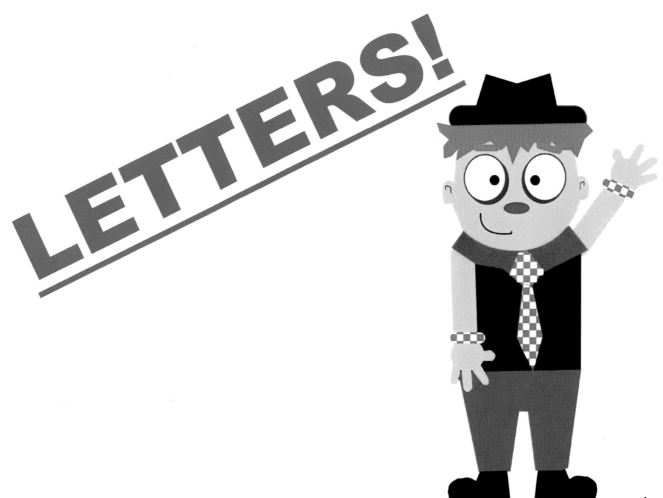

My buddy knows that

Starts with...

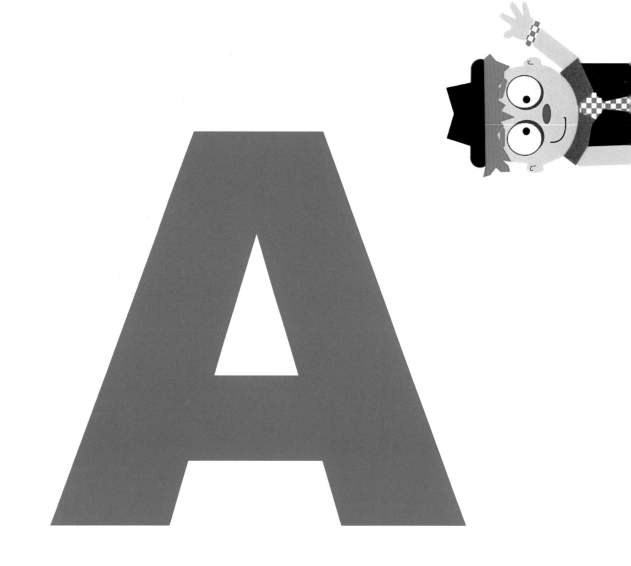

Apple starts with A.

My buddy knows that

Starts with...

Ball starts with B.

My buddy knows that

Starts with...

C

Car starts with C.

My buddy knows that

Fido

Starts with...

Dog starts with D.

My buddy knows that

Starts with...

Elephant starts with E.

My buddy knows that

Starts with...

Frog starts with F.

My buddy knows that

Starts with...

Goat starts with G.

My buddy knows that

Starts with...

Hat starts with H.

My buddy knows that

Starts with...

Ice Cream starts with I.

My buddy knows that

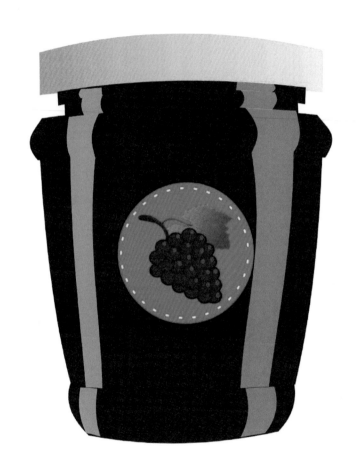

Starts with...

Jar starts with J.

My buddy knows that

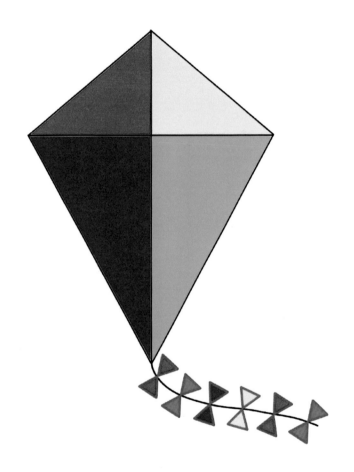

Starts with...

Kite starts with K.

My buddy knows that

Starts with...

Lion starts with L.

My buddy knows that

Starts with...

Monkey starts with M.

My buddy knows that

Starts with...

N

Nest starts with N.

My buddy knows that

Starts with...

Owl starts with O.

My buddy knows that

Starts with...

P

Pineapple starts with P.

My buddy knows that

Starts with...

Queen starts with Q.

My buddy knows that

Starts with...

Rocket starts with R.

My buddy knows that

Starts with...

Snake starts with S.

My buddy knows that

Starts with...

Turtle starts with T.

My buddy knows that

Starts with...

Umbrella starts with U.

My buddy knows that

Starts with...

Violin starts with V.

My buddy knows that

Starts with...

Walrus starts with W.

My buddy knows that

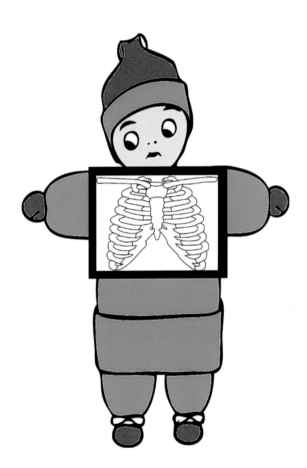

Starts with...

X-ray starts with X.

My buddy knows that

Starts with...

Yo-yo starts with Y.

My buddy knows that

Starts with...

Zebra starts with Z.

My buddy knows a lot about LETTERS!

Now, you do too!

Stay tuned for more My Buddy Knows Books...

Made in the USA
Lexington, KY
26 May 2018